Praying through Poetry: Hope for Violent Times

PEGGY ROSENTHAL

ST. ANTHONY MESSENGER PRESS

Cincinnati, Ohio

Scripture citations are taken from the *New Revised Standard Version Bible*, copyright ©1989 by the Division of Christian Education of the National Council of Churches of Christ in the U.S.A. and used by permission.

Cover and book design by Mark Sullivan

Earlier versions of Chapters One, Two and Three appeared in *The Christian Century, 2002.*

Other permissions to reprint previously published material may be found on page 83.

ISBN 0-86716-520-0

Library of Congress Cataloging-in-Publication Data

Rosenthal, Peggy.
  Praying through poetry : hope for violent times / Peggy Rosenthal.
     p. cm.
   ISBN 0-86716-520-0 (pbk.)
  1. Poetry, Modern-20th century. 2. Poetry, Modern-20th
century-History and criticism. 3. Religion and poetry. I. Title.
   PN6110.R4R64 2003
   811'.54080384--dc21
                                   2003004596

Published by St. Anthony Messenger Press
www.AmericanCatholic.org
Printed in the U.S.A.

Contents

Preface

It is difficult
to get the news from poems
yet men die miserably every day
for lack
of what is found there.
—*William Carlos Williams, "Asphodel, That Greeny Flower"*

In the numbness after September 11, 2001, I found that only the arts could lift my spirit. I craved classical music and went to concert after concert throughout the fall. I'd take an afternoon off to go and sit in front of a painting in the museum, planting myself on the floor and letting my gaze soak in the art and be soaked in by it. And, especially, I read and meditated with poetry, grateful for the way its language and imagery "reach comfortably into experience"—as poet Naomi Shihab Nye has said—"holding and connecting it more successfully than any news channel we could name."[1]

Our times, alas, are not rid of violence. September 11, 2001, was neither the start of our violent epoch, nor its finish. Where can we find our hope in such times? In prayer, yes, of course. But it isn't always clear what we should be asking of God, or of ourselves. What is most insidious about violence is that it traps both its victims and its perpetrators into the illusion that it is the way out of its own evil. Just this one act more of brute force, violence tells us, and you'll be safe. Just this one spell more of oppression, and you'll be free. And so violence sucks us—mind and spirit—into its world, as into an all-surrounding dark chaos. It stifles our ability to imagine anything but itself.

In 1984, when the Cold War threatened nuclear disaster, psychiatrist Robert Jay Lifton and psychologist Nicholas Humphrey compiled a book called *In a Dark Time: Images for Survival*. In it they explained the role of the creative imagination in our very ability to survive. "Human wisdom," they wrote, "has been the wisdom of the seer: the poet, painter, or peasant revolutionary, who, when the current world failed, turned the kaleidoscope of his or her imagination until familiar things took on a wholly different pattern. Such can and must be our imaginative strategy now."[2]

Here is where I find hope in violent times: in the seers whom God has blessed with the vision and courage to turn the kaleidoscopes of their imagination to show us new patterns to live by. Their creativity can take many forms: an initiative of individuals to engage in constructive projects with people whom their government has declared to be enemies; a commitment by a business to link its investments in a poor country to specific programs for bettering people's lives; the bold voice of a political leader who (imagine!) asks forgiveness of a group or nation whom his policies have harmed; the artful movement of a symphony or a film or a poem.

For this book, it is poems that I have gathered, poems that offer me a way to hope. Poetry is a medium especially suited to transformative vision, I think. Poetry's material—language—is already the medium of our constant communication: of the public rhetoric we hear from journalists and politicians and preachers, of our everyday conversation and thought, of worship and prayer. So poetry can take this most common stuff of life and imagine the uncommon through it, imagine new worlds that already are formed from our own and hence appear possible. As Archbishop of Canterbury Rowan Williams has put it, poetry creates a new "possible world, a reality in which my human reality can also find itself: and in inviting me into its world, the [poem] breaks open and extends my own possibilities."[3]

My purpose in this little book is to offer you some concrete experiences of poetry's world-creating possibilities. Each chapter introduces and then quotes in full a poem that somehow represents, for me, a way to hope in violent times. I encourage you to read the poem slowly and to sit quietly with it before going further, letting the visual design aid you in settling into the poem.

Next, I ask of the poem: *how does it lead me to hope?* To answer this question, I accept the poem's invitation to enter its world, and I enter by "thinking aloud" so that you can join me. I move through the poem, letting the force of its imaging carry me along. I let the reality that it envisions become mine, so that whatever possibilities it offers of breaking open the grip of violence on our times become my possibilities, and your possibilities, as well.

Any hope the poem has brought me to by its end will naturally lead me to prayer. Just as violence has the power to numb our spirits so dreadfully that we can't even picture what God wants of us, the freed imagination has the power to reenliven our relation to God. *So I might pray* with an image of the poem that has particularly struck me. Or I might pray with a relevant passage from the Bible or the Qur'an, or from a spiritual classic or a contemporary theologian or poet. Or I might pray with a few lines from another poem. All these movements toward prayer are meant to be merely suggestive: to invite you into whatever prayer the poem lifts you to.

I close each chapter with a final reflection, and then the suggestion to settle once more into a point or image in the poem that has particularly moved you: *Returning to the poem one more time, is there an image I want to sit with in prayer, in hope?* You might want at this time to copy out or even memorize that piece of the poem, so that its hope and prayer can remain with you.

The ten poems around which these chapters are built were drawn from a wealth of verse written in the context of our recent decades of world violence. Understandably, much poetry responding to violence is quite grim. I haven't ignored such poems, but always I've looked for ones that offer at least a glimpse of *hope* for violent times. And I've chosen poems that speak in a range of tones, from near despair to calm meditation to playful fun. I've looked for variety, as well, in the poets' religious traditions; represented are poets from Christian, Muslim, Jewish and Buddhist backgrounds.

Though I've arranged the chapters so as to hint at suggestive juxtapositions between poems, the chapters are independent and can really be read in any order.

Each of the ten poems moves us, I believe, because its author has been moved in the course of composing it. We tend to think of poetry as "personal" or "private," but a great poem on a public theme is compelling to read because it was personally compelling for the poet to write. "Poets write poems from the same impulse that others read them," said poet Denise Levertov, pondering what motivated her to devote decades of her career to composing so-called "political" poems.

> People turn to poems (if they are aware poetry
> exists) for some kind of illumination, for
> revelations that help them to survive, to survive
> in spirit not only in body. . . . It is when I feel
> the political/social issues personally that I'm
> moved to write of them, in just the same spirit of
> quest, of talking to myself in quest of revelation
> or illumination, that is a motivating force for
> more obviously "personal" poems. . . . And if
> they can so function for the writer, then they
> have a chance of doing so for the reader. The
> writer is given a voice to articulate what many
> others feel but can't say.[4]

Sometimes, in the face of our society's deeply entrenched violence, Levertov had to talk herself into keeping her creative spirit up. Yet, even at her lowest she could find images of hope because she believed in poetry's genuine life-changing power. Urging herself onward in the dark time of the Cold War, she exhorted herself (and us) in a poem called "Writing in the Dark":

> Keep writing in the dark:
> a record of the night, or
> words that pulled you from depths of unknowing, . . .
>
> or opened
> as flowers of a tree that blooms
> only once in a lifetime:
>
> words that may have the power
> to make the sun rise again.

NOTES

[1] Naomi Shihab Nye, *19 Varieties of Gazelle: Poems of the Middle East* (New York: HarperCollins, 2002), p. xvi.

[2] Robert Jay Lifton and Nicholas Humphrey, *In a Dark Time: Images for Survival* (Cambridge, Md.: Harvard University Press, 1984), p. 3.

[3] Rowan Williams, "Trinity and Revelation," *On Christian Theology* (London: Blackwell, 2000), p. 133.

[4] Denise Levertov, "Poetry, Prophecy, Survival," *New & Selected Essays* (New York: New Directions, 1992), p. 150.

Chapter One
'You See the World Lit Differently'

In violent times, I'm drawn especially to recent Polish poetry. Poland suffered a half-century of violence, from the Nazi occupation to Communist totalitarian oppression and terror. Out of this collective national experience, Polish poets like Adam Zagajewski have developed a voice and vision of wise reflection on the interchange between public evils and the individual human heart.

The Greenhouse

In a small black town, your town,
where even trains linger unwilling,
anxious to be on their way,
in a park, defying soot and shadows,
a gray building stands lined with mother-of-pearl.

Forget the snow, the frost's repeated blows;
inside you're greeted by a damp anthology of breezes
and the enigmatic whispers of vast leaves
coiled like lazy snakes. Even an Egyptologist
couldn't make them out.

Forget the sadness of dark stadiums and streets,
the weight of thwarted Sundays.
Accept the warm breath wafting from the plants.
The gentle scent of faded lightning
engulfs you, beckoning you on.

Perhaps you see the rust sails of ships at port,
islands snared in rosy mist, crumbling temples' towers;
you glimpse what you've lost, what never was,
and people with lives like your own.

Suddenly you see the world lit differently,
other people's doors swing open for a moment,
you read their hidden thoughts, their holidays don't hurt,
their happiness is less opaque, their faces
almost beautiful.

Lose yourself, go blind from ecstasy,
forgetting everything, and then perhaps
a deeper memory, a deeper recognition will return,
and you'll hear yourself saying: I don't know how—
the palm trees opened up my greedy heart.

—*Adam Zagajewski*

How does the poem lead me to hope?

The poem starts me off in a world of sinister darkness. The anonymous town—"your" town, the poet insists, putting me at once into the poem's world—is so black, sooty, shadowy, that even trains passing through get the creeps and are anxious to leave. Yet the glimmer of a brighter world is offered at the stanza's very end: the inside walls of a gray building (a greenhouse, we know from the title) are "mother-of pearl."

"Forget the snow," the poet suddenly commands me; forget the bitter cold blows of the outside world. "Inside" the greenhouse is where he takes me: to its lush greeting of a fanciful "anthology of breezes" and the whispering welcome of "vast leaves." There's a mystery in here, the poet hints, but it seems exotically intriguing rather than threatening.

The poet's contrasting commands continue in stanza three. I'm ordered to "forget" the outside world's dark sadness and weight. (Are "Sundays" particularly "thwarted," I wonder, because they're the day of the Resurrection, of light and hope?) "Stadiums," "streets" and the "Sundays" hinting at church-going: these are images of places where people should joyfully gather. Yet in this dark town, all communal delight has been thwarted by an unnamed dread. So the poet urges me to "accept" instead the healing "warm breath wafting" from the greenhouse plants.

He himself initiates this process of "forgetting" harsh outside realities, as he sinks his poetic senses into the alluring sound, feel and scent of the greenhouse's alternate world, "beckoning you on."

On to where, I wonder. But already he is leading me there—tentatively, gently— with his "perhaps" which opens the next verse. Where I'm beckoned, I find, is into the world of the free imagination: sailing ships, rosy mists, a fantasy world of "what never was." And through imagination's realm, I'm brought to "people with lives like your own."

Coming to these people is a double jolt. First, I'd never have expected to arrive, by way of fantasy, at real people like me. Second, it hits me that to this point there have been no people in the poem. The only life in the poem, I now see, had come from objects (the anxious trains) or the greenhouse's protected environment (whispering leaves and welcoming breezes). But now, glimpses of longed for or lost dream worlds have dissolved the barrier between outer and inner worlds that dominated the poem's first half. Being able to imagine idealized worlds allows us to break through the dreadful dark isolation of an oppressive reality, to a new reality promising hope because it is peopled with our own soul mates. That's what the poem dramatizes in this, its revelatory moment.

From this instant, all darkness vanishes from the poem. "You see the world lit differently." And in this new light, this new light-heartedness, images of the possibility of human community are released to rush in: delightful images of "people's doors swinging open for a moment," so that "you read their hidden thoughts," and—marvelous image of freedom from envy and fear—"their holidays don't hurt."

How wildly wonderful is this loss of isolation. The poem makes me smile with its giddy vision of radical human connectedness. "Lose yourself," the poet gleefully shouts, and I hear an echo of the Gospel injunction to radical self-abandonment. "Go blind from ecstasy" so that you can start seeing totally afresh. Let yourself be dispossessed of "everything" that you were so sure you understood. And then, in this utter emptiness of blessed forgetfulness, deeper truths have a chance to slip in: "a deeper memory, a deeper recognition" of human oneness. "And you'll hear yourself saying," in the hush now of a prayer, "I don't know how— / the palm trees opened up my greedy heart."

And so I might pray—

- I might pray by meditating on the wonder disclosed in this final image. "I don't know how" such human transformation happens—my greedy heart opened up by palm trees!—but I trust that it does. The poem has renewed this trust, by taking me through an experience of transformation's mystery.
- I might pray in thanksgiving for poetry's gift of opening up our words and worlds, so that the transformative experience in the greenhouse can be a symbol of possibility for each of our hearts and for our nation or the entire globe. For, as another Polish poet, Nobel Prize winner Czeslaw Milosz, puts it in a poem called "Ars Poetica?":

> The purpose of poetry is to remind us
> how difficult it is to remain just one person,
> for our house is open, there are no keys in the doors,
> and invisible guests come in and out at will.

- I might pray with the opening image of another poem, "For the Unknown Enemy," by American poet William

Stafford, which shares Zagajewski's vision of how liberating it is to see others' lives lit differently, so "their holidays don't hurt":

> This monument is for the unknown
> good in our enemies. Like a picture
> their life began to appear: they
> gathered at home in the evening
> and sang. Above their fields they saw
> a new sky. A holiday came
> and they carried the baby to the park
> for a party. . . .

And, finally, I might ponder what editor Gregory Wolfe wrote in *Image: A Journal of the Arts and Religion.*

> Art, like religious faith in general and prayer in particular, has the power to help us transcend the fragmented society we inhabit....The imagination calls us to leave our personalities behind and to temporarily inhabit another's experience, thus allowing us to look at the world with new eyes. Art invites us to meet the Other—whether that be our neighbor or the infinite otherness of God—and to achieve a new wholeness of spirit.[1]

Returning to the poem one more time, is there an image I want to sit with in prayer, in hope?

NOTES
[1] Gregory Wolfe, "Art, Faith, and the Stewardship of Culture," *Image #25* (Winter 1999–2000), p. 100.

Chapter Two

'My Body Opens into Brothers'

Lucille Clifton is an African American poet whose consciousness of her race and gender inform all of her poetry, though she never gets preachy. Instead, she writes in a minimalist mode that clears out human society's clutter, the mess we've made by identifying ourselves in contending genders, ethnicities, nations. The first thing that strikes a reader of Clifton's poetry is what is missing: capitalization, punctuation, long and plentiful lines. We see a poetry so pared down that its spaces take on substance, become a shaping presence as much as the words themselves. And we see a radically egalitarian world where no capitalized word lords it over others. Clifton is a master of poetry's art of saying much with little. She likes to compose very short poems, often clustering them in thematic or narrative groupings. Here are the first two of a sequence called "some jesus": sixteen spare poems each reflecting on a key biblical moment.

adam and eve

the names
of the things
bloom in my mouth

my body opens
into brothers

cain

the land of nod
is a desert
on my head   i
plant tears
every morning
my brother
don't rise up

—*Lucille Clifton*

How do the poems lead me to hope?

The title words of the first poem, "adam and eve,"
immediately make me see our first parents afresh. Without
capital letters, they look humbled, on the same plane as
everything else in the poem's world. It's the world at the start

of Genesis, of course. But the poet chooses to enter the Bible's creation account at a particular point, where God gives Adam the power to name all the animals and birds.

The stanza enacts its own creation process, expanding from a line of only two words to a line of three, then of four. Step by developing step, it moves into the image of "blooming." I gasp when I reach this metaphor, my own mouth opened in an "Ah!" like Adam's. Here is an image of humanity so in harmony with the rest of creation that our power over it is as a blooming in our mouths: we don't order it around or command it to do our will; rather, we let its essence speak through us.

With no period to block the flow at the end of the sentence, "my mouth" seems to transmute—in the space between the stanzas—into "my body," which "opens" like another blooming. Human reproduction is imaged as a natural opening "into brothers": into the brothers Cain and Abel, yes, but also into the brothers of "my body." The poet has crafted this ambiguity of "brothers" so that they're at once the next generation and also all humankind as a single family, all brothers of Eve.

Or of Adam? Here is another subtly crafted ambiguity: the poet won't let me be sure whether "my body" belongs to Adam or to Eve, or to them both. "My mouth" in stanza one seemed to be Adam's, since he does the naming in Genesis. "My body" would seem to be Eve's, the woman's body opening in childbirth. So who, I have to wonder, is the poem's speaker? The title hints that it is both "adam and eve," jointly. That transmutation of "my mouth" into "my body" suggests the same. Without making a fuss, simply by the art of arranging a few chosen words, the poet dissolves the gender break that has historically distorted so much of human relations. Gender is irrelevant, she implies. Try looking at the world without it, man and woman as one flesh and one spirit: naming, reproducing, cocreating.

The poem "adam and eve" is so short that I can review it now in a glance. I can see that its visual shape is itself an image: the whole poem looks like a single deep breath. Stanza one expands as an inhalation, stanza two exhales, so that the whole is a breath of creative life that is the poem's very being, its meaning.

With this deep breath of life in mind, in my body, I move on to the next poem, "cain." And my breath at once turns into heaves of sobbing: each line of "cain" seems a disconnected gasp of anguished sorrow. Having broken natural human bonds by killing, Cain can't share in his parents' life-enhancing breath. There's no blooming for him; the only cultivation he knows is to plant fruitless tears of remorse.

He has been banished, Genesis 4:16 tells us, to the land of Nod, a word which means "wandering." The poet dramatizes Cain's displacement by cutting loose his grammatical moorings. Phrases like "on my head" and "every morning" wander rootlessly: is the desert on my head? or on my head do i plant tears? do i plant tears every morning? or is it that every morning my brother don't rise up? The absence of punctuation—which for "adam and eve" both represents and facilitates their harmonious merging—for "cain" is the mark and message of disorientation.

But the sign of the poet's Cain that is most heartbreaking is that small "i" hanging alone out in the poem's space. It reminds me of what theologian Rowan Williams said in a sermon during the Gulf War, years before he became archbishop of Canterbury: "Violent human conflict is the effect of the steady shrinkage of the world to the dimensions of the ego. It is *my* interests that interpret and process what I see, and yours can increasingly appear only as a rival bid for the territory I have colonized." Lucille Clifton hints at something like this ego-aggrandizement as the cause of Cain's murderous act, for his punishment is an ego now shrunk to an isolated little "i," cut off from all bonding with others or the earth.

Rereading "adam and eve" and "cain" together, I see that Clifton has re-envisioned the origin of human sinfulness and suffering. Sin, as she views it, enters the world not with Eve and Adam, but with violence against "my brother."

So the poems as a pair offer me a choice of ways to be with my brother, that is, with every other person on God's earth. I can be with my brother in blooming, or I can be with him in tears that tear (rip, slash) him apart. My body can open into him, or it can close him out, annihilating him so that he "don't rise up." I can be with him in the garden, in hope, or I can be with him in the desert, in murderous violence.

And so I might pray—

• I might pray with Pope John XXIII, in his encyclical *Pacem in Terris* (¶171), that the Prince of Peace

>   banish from human hearts whatever might
>   endanger peace. May He transform them into
>   witnesses of truth, justice, and brotherly love....

May He enkindle the wills of all so that they
may overcome the barriers that divide, cherish
the bonds of mutual charity, understand
others, and pardon those who have done them
wrong. By virtue of His action, may all
peoples of the earth become as brothers, and
may the most longed-for peace blossom forth
and reign always among them.

- I might pray with this verse from a poem by Jane
  Hirshfield, "October 20, 1983," which also offers, like
  Lucille Clifton's pair of poems, the metaphor of gardening
  as an image of hope, juxtaposed with an ominous sense of
  the terrifying consequences we head for if we quarrel
  outside the garden:

  > For the winter garden
  > roses are pruned and carefully tied,
  > earth banked up over the roots.
  > What if after Antigone, the moment of catharsis,
  > we quarrel in the car going home?
  > If compassion cannot cure us?
  > What if we fail?

- I might pray with the New Testament's letter of James
  (1:19–21), which warns us against imitating Cain's rush to
  angry violence. "Let everyone be quick to listen, slow to
  speak, slow to anger; for your anger does not produce God's
  righteousness. Therefore rid yourselves of all sordidness
  and rank growth of wickedness, and welcome with
  meekness the implanted word that has the power to save

your souls." May God's word planted in our hearts find fertile soil.

And, finally, I might ponder how Pastor Kate Gussey, the central character of Erin McGraw's novel *The Baby Tree*, gratefully looks back at her religious conversion:

> Maybe it was grace, maybe pure chance. But I
> started to see a new world, a system that I hadn't
> seen before. People were all connected, lifting
> one another up or tearing down. Everybody
> doing one or the other. The whole universe was
> being created and destroyed at the same time,
> every minute. Once I started to see that, I
> wanted to be one who lifted.[1]

Kate's vision is Lucille Clifton's, I see. At every minute the whole universe is being created with "eve" and being destroyed with "cain." And at every minute I can participate as a creator or a destroyer. I can be Cain, tearing down my brother so he "don't rise up." Or I can try, with God's grace, to help him rise.

With Kate, with Clifton's "eve," I want to be—I pray that I may be—one who "lifts."

Returning to the poem one more time, is there an image I want to sit with in prayer, in hope?

NOTES
[1] Erin McGraw, *The Baby Tree* (Ashland, Ore.: Story Line Press, 2002), p. 37.

Chapter Three

'I Set Jim Free'

For Christians, our hope in violent times—in all times—is
Christ. But what exactly does that mean? Poet Scott Cairns
gives us a delightfully fresh approach to this crucial question
through the voice of a comic character he invented who is
named Raimundo Luz. Raimundo is indeed a character:
supposedly a Portuguese postmodernist theologian, whose
series of autobiographical verses Cairns pretends to be
translating, Luz breezily discourses from various stances. In
the poem of the series called "My Imitation," Cairns has Luz
take on the time-honored journey of the *Imitation of Christ*,
based on the (real) fourteenth-century Christian classic of
that title. While some poems are meant to be mulled over in
quiet solitude, this is one that begs to be read aloud. Tone is
everything in Luz's "Imitation." The fun comes from the
disjunction between the speaker's deadpan account and our
recognition, in his flatly presented details, of deeper truths
that he appears not to notice.

The Translation of Raimundo Luz: My Imitation

I sold my possessions, even the colorful pencils.
I gave all my money to the dull. I gave my poverty
to the president. I became a child again, naked
and relatively innocent. I let the president have my guilt.

I found a virgin and asked her to be my mother.
She held me very sweetly.

I watched father build beautiful shapes with wood.
He too had a gentle way.

I made conversation in holy places with the chosen.
Their theater was grim.

I suggested they cheer up. Many repented,
albeit elaborately.

I floated the wide river on a raft.
I set Jim free.

I revised every word.

One morning, very early, I was taken by brutes and
    beaten.
I was nailed to a cross so sturdy I thought
father himself might have shaped it.

I gestured for a cool drink and was mocked.
I took on the sins of the world and regretted my
    extravagance.
I gave up and died. I descended into hell
and spoke briefly with the president.

I rose again, bloodless and feeling pretty good.

I forgave everything.

—*Scott Cairns*

How does the poem lead me to hope?

Raimundo Luz starts off his imitation of Christ, fittingly, with a string of dispossessions. Each begins by sounding like standard Gospel fare, then takes an incongruous twist that makes me smile. "I sold my possessions"; yes, sell all you have, the Gospel tells us. But "colorful pencils" sound inappropriately trivial as one's prized possession—unless Luz is a simpleton or a child. "I gave all my money"; yes, sell all you have and give to the poor. Oops, no. Raimundo chooses "the dull," as if dullness had the greatest need (of those colorful pencils perhaps?). Now his possession is poverty itself, so he's ready to give that away as well—"to the president"—and I chuckle that, yes, the president (any president) could use some poverty. "I became a child again"; yes, to such as these belongs the kingdom of God. But now the twist is that the child is only "relatively" innocent. And the final dispossession: of "guilt"—again "to the president." I grin knowingly: here's something the president (any president) already has in abundance.

I'm coming to see Raimundo Luz as an ingénue. In his relative innocence he speaks more wisely than he knows. All these dispossessions, I can see looking back, are in fact marvelously appropriate as an imitation of Christ's radical self-emptying at the Incarnation: Christ Jesus "emptied himself, taking the form of a slave, being born in human likeness" (Philippians 2:7). Colorful pencils in this context now look like heaven's joy, which Christ gave up for our sakes.

I follow Luz now down the steps of his imitation of Christ's life as narrated in the Gospels. And the steps, each a single stanza, do look visually like a series of steps or platforms—except that each teeters on a short line underneath that trips me for an instant. What makes me stumble and grab on tight is Raimundo's wry comic angle on each stage of the Gospel story. Yet I'm following him through recognizable Gospel places—Jesus' birth and childhood, his encounters with Pharisees and with repentent sinners —until we suddenly land on "the wide river on a raft" and "set Jim free."

I do a double take: how did we ever get from the Bible into *Huckleberry Finn?* Clearly the poet, in making this wild leap, wants me to ponder precisely this question. And he has plunked us into this particular scene from Mark Twain's novel—where Huck is defying his society's laws by escorting the slave Jim down the river to freedom—at the exact middle of the poem, making Huck's exploit literally central to the imitation of Christ.

So I pause on the raft and ponder. Here is Raimundo Luz imitating Huck Finn, the innocent child who challenges society's conventions by doing radical good despite himself.

Yes, this is consistent with Luz's character as I've come to know it. So, then, in imitating Huck, is Luz still imitating Christ? Yes, of course: all at once the apparent incongruity of Huck's raft floating through the Gospels dissolves. I see Jesus for what he truly is throughout the Gospels: the radical innocent overturning conventions, setting us free from whatever attitudes, opinions, supposed certainties enslave us.

And then I leap with Luz off the raft into the one-line stanza: "I revised every word." Naturally my instinct is to ask: every word of what? But the poet has led me to frame a different sort of question. By now I know that he is giving us, through Luz, a re-interpretation of Jesus' own life and meaning. So he leads me to ask: okay, how is "revising every word" what Jesus did? And all the Gospel re-visings rush in: "the greatest among you must become like the youngest"; "you have heard it said 'an eye for an eye . . . ,' but I say to you, Do not resist an evil doer"; "you have heard it said 'you shall love your neighbor and hate your enemy,' but I say to you, Love your enemies and pray for those who persecute you." Suddenly this one short line of the poem is exploding with the entire Gospel message of Jesus the radical revisionist.

The poem then takes me to exactly where revising every word took Jesus: to suffering the violence of the Crucifixion. Without a blink, Luz folds his inadvertent jokes into his disarmingly bland Passion narrative. The blandness is tongue-in-cheek on the poet's part, of course. In Raimundo's cool tone, the poet manages to blend the deadly seriousness of the Passion with a matter-of-fact shrug that says, sure, beatings and mockery and defeat are the Christian life, what do you expect?

Finally, "I forgave everything," Raimundo simply announces. In his innocence, he takes Christ at his word. Forgive seventy times seven. I laugh at Raimundo's extravagance (which he has "regretted" but not abandoned). But I know the joke is on me, on us: if we aren't equally extravagant, we're not imitating Christ.

The hope to which the poem has led me is a lightness of heart even in the midst of violence. By laughing, I can feel the joy at the core of the Christian challenge. I acknowledge the crazy wildness, and the risks, of trying to imitate Christ. Can I really set Jim free, though civil disobedience for a moral cause could bring me to jail or worse? Can I revise (reenvision, look anew at) every opinion I hold dear? If I'm "taken by brutes and beaten"—whether literally or with harsh unjust words—can I still forgive everything? *Everything?* Raimundo makes me see how daunting a true imitation of Christ must be, and yet how astonishingly necessary. And since Jesus rose "feeling pretty good," I can hope I will too.

And so I might pray—

- I might pray to have just a bit of Raimundo's spirit, or the spirit of another poetic character—the "Mad Farmer" invented by Wendell Berry—who also voices the wild upside down commandments of Jesus, to overturn our natural instincts of grim anger, of resentment, of counting the costs:

    So, friends, every day do something
    that won't compute. Love the Lord.

> Love the world. Work for nothing.
> Take all that you have and be poor.
> Love someone who does not deserve it. . . .
> Expect the end of the world. Laugh.
> Laughter is immeasurable. Be joyful
> though you have considered all the facts.

- I might pray by singing daily the hymn "I Danced in the Morning," where Jesus romps through his life story as Lord of the Dance, urging us to follow his lead.

- I might pray with Pope John Paul II in his World Peace Day message of January 1, 2002, that in

> a world in which the power of evil seems once again to have taken the upper hand, the shattered order cannot be fully restored except by a response that combines justice with forgiveness. . . . Forgiveness is a personal choice, a decision of the heart to go against the natural instinct to pay back evil with evil. . . . It has its perfect exemplar in the forgiveness of Christ, who on the cross prayed, "Father, forgive them; for they know not what they do."

And, finally, I might ponder the way another contemporary poet, the Anglican priest R. S. Thomas, envisions Jesus emptying himself in order to give us hope. In "The Coming," Thomas imagines Jesus in heaven before the Incarnation, looking down at the scorched earth where "a bright Serpent, a river / uncoiled itself, radiant / with slime."

                On a bare
Hill a bare tree saddened
The sky. Many people
Held out their thin arms
To it, as though waiting
For a vanished April
To return to its crossed
Boughs. The son watched
Them. Let me go there, he said.

*Returning to the poem one more time, is there an image I want to
sit with in prayer, in hope?*

Chapter Four
'With Such a Good Fit'

Contemporary U.S. poet Jane Hirshfield writes out of her spiritual formation in Zen Buddhist practice. "Zen taught me how to pay attention," she has said, "how to delve, how to question and enter, how to stay with—or at least want to try to stay with—whatever is going on." Once asked how the practice of Zen and the writing of poetry were related for her, she replied that in both "experience comes first. My job as a human being as well as a writer is to feel as thoroughly as possible the experience that I am part of, and then press it a little further. To find out what happens if I ask, 'What else, what next, what more, what deeper, what hidden?'"[1]

On the Current Events

The shadows of countries are changing,
like the figures in the dreams of a long sickness.

Argentina, which used to be so full of sunlight
and heroic, whistling pampas cowboys.
Greece, the lovely heifer of curving horns.
Thailand, Palestine, Salvador.

Of course, it is not this constant thing, history,
but ourselves,
like the wooden statue of some sacred figure,
wormed through,

with the bitter aftertaste on the heart
of too much coffee,
any evening,
after too much talk of unimportant things,

when all of it is important:
the cup placed with such a good fit
on its saucer, well and carefully made,
all the still-pieced pieces of our shared consent.

—*Jane Hirshfield*

How does the poem lead me to hope?

There is a quiet about this poem, which the title doesn't
prepare me for. "Current events" tend to be noisy clashes of
opinions or arms, and discourse "on" them (whether from
media pundits or callers to radio talk shows) usually picks up

their contentious tone. But Hirshfield refuses to enter the fray. Instead, she reflects "on the current events" as if from afar, starting from an imagined distance so high that countries seem to cast "shadows," and we don't hear a sound. The silence is ominous, though; things are not well. "The shadows of countries are changing, / like the figures in the dreams of a long sickness." Countries, which we expect to remain solid, fixed entities, here seem to be losing their forms in the fevered suffering of bad dreams.

The poet moves us closer in, now, to particular countries, presumably ones that are suffering from "current events." She pictures what these countries have changed *from*—but in images so idealized, so filled with a hushed nostalgia, that she makes us doubt that they ever were real. A sun-filled, whistling Argentina and a lovely heifered Greece are the lands of fantasy. So she doesn't even need to paint details for what "used to be" Thailand, Palestine, Salvador. We can fill in their pastel-colored stories as well as she.

From the opening stanza's sense of overcast shadows, of bad dreams weighing heavily on the present, the poem has switched to the overlit nostalgic dreams of an illusory past. And then with the next stanza, the tone shifts again. Still quiet, it is now the voice of "of course," the voice of reason and common sense. What the poet calmly and reasonably states in this line, however, stops me cold, as she means it to. All this fluidity of countries, their changes in the "current" of "current events," flowing from dream to dream, from wishful fantasy to nightmare and back: she characterizes this flux as the "constant thing" that is "history." I'm numbed by the depressing implications of this picture of "history," as a sliding among delusions and nothing more.

But there is a possibly hopeful note in this line: the word "not." However constant the shiftiness of history, the poem states unequivocally that "it is not." Not *what*? Not what matters? Not what is real? This is the sense of the thought that is left uncompleted, held suspended as the poem gently drops us into what *is*—

"But ourselves." With these words, set off on their own line, the poem has landed, I feel, on its true subject. Ourselves. Yet we're not even mid-way through the poem. What will follow? How will it continue? The poet has told us her creative process: "to feel as thoroughly as possible the experience that I am part of, and then press it a little further." So she will press on into "ourselves." She will "delve . . . enter . . . stay with" the experience of being "ourselves." She will press on "to find out what happens if I ask, 'What else, what next, what more, what deeper, what hidden?'"

What more is, first, a simile: what we ourselves are like. "Like the wooden statue of some sacred figure." It is not a flattering image. To be like a statue might be lovely, except that the "wooden" makes us sound unresponsive and stiff. And to be formed like a "sacred figure" might be good, except that the tone of the word "some" discounts this value, as if shrugging "oh, it's some god or other." Worse yet, dropping into the next line, we find ourselves "wormed through." We are being eaten away at, the image tells us, as if carrying in our beings that "long sickness" of our shadowy countries.

What exactly has wormed us through? The poem drops us, again—delicately, on the breath between stanzas—as the poet delves further into her images, looking to see "what else, what hidden?" The image she finds is not a pleasant one: "the bitter aftertaste on the heart / of too much coffee." So, then, a stimulant overdone has left us bitter to the core. Dropping further, into "any evening," we enter the ordinary round of our normal lives. But still more is wrong here: "too much talk of unimportant things." Here is our everyday social life, our apparently innocent after-dinner chitchat with family and friends, presented by the poem as an image of what worms through the potential sacredness of "ourselves."

And we're not through; the poem quietly presses on. The sentence (three whole stanzas it will take) has more to go. "What more, what deeper, what hidden?" And here, at the start of the last stanza, it finally reaches a turn to the positive, a tone of uplift: "when all of it is important." All? It? These are large terms. The poet is making her grand sweep, a gesture of: here, dear readers, is what we have been waiting for. Here is everything that matters in life!

I'm on pins and needles to press on past the colon, to discover what the all-important "it" can be. So I'm astounded to find that it is simply a single cup and saucer. I stare. Right in the midst of "any evening," *this* is what matters: "the cup placed with such a good fit / on its saucer, well and carefully made."

The image holds me with absolute attention. This most common, small domestic thing, a cup on its saucer: how can it be of greater import than the sickly changing countries of current events? By being placed "with such a good fit," the poem tells me; by being "well and carefully made." The import is in the artisan's craft, in the making of objects with an attentive "care" which resonates of moral value: which is "well" and "good."

The image holds me, yet the comma at the line's end drops me gently into the poem's last line. What lies deeper, hidden, next? Immediately, another "all." The word folds me back to the "all" at the start of the stanza, the two *alls* now enfolding the well-crafted cup and saucer. "All . . . all": the poet repeats her insistence that, amazing as it seems, a single well-made cup placed with good fit on its saucer is "all."

All of what, though? Pressing a little further into this most particular of images, and then a bit further into each image to which she arrives, the poet moves through an ever-doubling sequence of words which ripple out to a general vision which unexpectedly returns us to "ourselves" made new and whole. That, at least, is how I see the extraordinary course of movement of the poem's final line. But I want to replay it now in slow motion, because I sense that the poet's way of experiencing her images is a model for our engaging our own "current events" in hope.

First we follow her into the double meaning of "still": quiet, and also ongoing. Then comes the blatantly repeated "pieces," their doubling making us pause and look closely at what they might hold. In the context of the cup and saucer, the pieces remind me of dishware: a set. But after the image of "a good fit," I think also of a puzzle, whose pieces we must find the right fit for.

With the preposition "of," the poem draws me into its final image of what is being pieced together into a set and a "good fit," and the words take me aback with their apparent abstractness: "our shared consent." Is the "our" everyone? It does seem to be inclusive of all humankind, like the earlier "ourselves." I want to ask, "shared consent" about what? But the poem won't let me; rather, it renders such a question irrelevant. It's not the *what* of shared consent that matters, but the *how*. Our shared consent is like an artisan's craft, the poem suggests: pieces pieced quietly and carefully together, well made. And reverberating out from the poet's re-toning of *pieced pieces*, I now hear an echo of "peace."

"Our shared consent": here is the poem's resting place of hope in the face of history's constantly shifting, sickly dream world. A truly shared consent, among all involved in "the current events" of the moment, would indeed move us away from whatever ills are plaguing our countries. The poem doesn't specify these ills as violent ones, but any shadow of a country over others is a form of violence: uninvited military occupation; economic pressures from giant companies, the terrifying shadow of a plane about to become or to drop a bomb. No one, no group or individual, wants to be under such a shadow; no one would freely consent to being violated in any way. Where a shared consent is "a good fit"—morally good, made "well," full of "care" for each "piece"—violence cannot be.

And so I might pray—

- I might pray with the figure of Wisdom from the Bible, who "is more mobile than any motion; because of her pureness she pervades and penetrates all things." In her there is "a spirit that is intelligent, holy, unique, manifold, subtle, mobile, clear, unpolluted, distinct, invulnerable,

loving the good, keen, irresistible, beneficent, humane,
steadfast, sure, free from anxiety, all-powerful, overseeing
all" (Wisdom of Solomon, 7:22–24). Surely here in
Wisdom's spirit are some "pieces of our shared consent."

- I might pray with this vignette from the Arab-American
poet Naomi Shihab Nye's "Passing the Refugee Camp":

> In the next town
> a man sets tea on our table
>
> He does not speak
> He glides from the kitchen
>
> a pot of steaming water
> a pot of steaming milk
>
> His brother has been beaten by soldiers
> He saw the blood come out of the nose
>
> Because of this he is walking
> very slowly so not one drop
>
> exceeds its edge

- I might pray with the Qur'an (42:36):

> That which you have been given is but the
> fleeting pleasure of this life. Better and more
> enduring is God's recompense to those who
> believe and put their trust in Him; who avoid
> grievous sins and lewd acts and, when
> angered, are willing to forgive; who obey their
> Lord, attend to their prayers, and conduct
> their affairs by mutual consent.

And, finally, I might ponder these lines from a poem called "Making Peace," by Denise Levertov:

> Peace, like a poem,
> is not there ahead of itself,
> can't be imagined before it is made,
> can't be known except in the words of its making....
> A feeling towards it,
> dimly sensing a rhythm, is all we have
> until we begin to utter its metaphors,
> learning them as we speak.

Returning to the poem one more time, is there an image I want to sit with in prayer, in hope?

NOTES
[1] Interview in *Atlantic Unbound* (*Atlantic Monthly* online), September 18, 1997.

Chapter Five

'Write Our Names in Crimson Vapor'

What can poetry do when the violence suffered by a people
seems past bearing? Sometimes a poet's only hope is to
articulate the horror, to witness to it with words that are
more than a shriek or a moan. Palestinian poets have taken
this as their task since 1948, when their people were expelled
from their homeland, their villages destroyed. Leading
among these poetic voices has been Mahmoud Darwish, a
Sunni Muslim born in one of the Palestinian villages which
was taken over by the Israelis after the 1948 war, when he
was six years old. His family fled to Lebanon, then returned
and settled in Galilee; since then Darwish has moved from
place to place, always identifying with his people's pained
sense of forced exile. He had been living in Beirut as
founding editor of a literary journal when the 1982 Israeli
invasion of Lebanon forced him out yet again. "Earth Scrapes
Us" was written in response to this incident, but the poem
speaks for any group of people, of any place or time, who feel
beaten into the ground.

Earth Scrapes Us

Earth scrapes us, pressing us into the last narrow passage,
  we have to dismember ourselves to pass,
Earth squeezes us. Wish we were its wheat, to die and live
  again. Wish it were our mother,
Our mother would be merciful to us. Wish we were images
  of stones that our dreams carry
Like mirrors. We have seen the faces of those who will be
  killed defending the soul to the last one of us.
We wept for the birthday of their children. We have seen
  the faces of those who will throw
Our children from the windows of this last space of ours.
  Mirrors that our star will paste together.
Where shall we go, after the last frontier? Where will
  birds be flying, after the last sky?
Where will plants find a place to rest, after the last
  expanse of air?
We will write our names in crimson vapor.
We will cut off the hand of song, so that our flesh can
  complete the song.
Here we will die. Here in the last narrow passage. Or here
  our blood will plant—its olive trees.

—*Mahmoud Darwish*

How does the poem lead me to hope?

Letting myself experience this poem's images won't be a
comfortable process. But I need to enter into them fully in
order to make sure that any hope I might be led to doesn't
slip too easily past the poem's core pain.

The poet has already brought me in, anyway, with the first
line, for it speaks of "us" and "we." A community of suffering
is what I'm (reluctantly) joining. Together, we are being
scraped, pressed, squeezed by the earth "into the last narrow
passage." I feel my breath being stifled, as if we're being
buried alive, horribly "dismembering ourselves to pass."

If this burial were like that of a grain of wheat, we could
hope for new life from it. If we were submerging in a true
Mother Earth, we could hope for mercy from her. The poet
articulates these wishes, and then one that's more perplexing:
"Wish we were images of stones that our dreams carry / Like
mirrors." I can't grasp this wish with my mind, but if I move
inside it I sense the longing for a reality that reflects the firm
and natural hope of our dreams, all humankind's dreams.

Then suddenly the images are all too clear. "The faces of
those who will be killed." "The birthday of their children."
"The faces of those who will throw"—what? bombs? That's
how my mind instinctively completes the line. But no, it is
unimaginably worse:—"throw / Our children from the
windows."

"…of this last space of ours." The claustrophobic sense of
being squeezed out of life continues. Is that why "mirrors"
appear again? "Mirrors that our star will paste together."
Mirrors are our hope for reflecting, connecting with a life
outside this dead-end trap. Having to work at visualizing this

unusual image exercises my mind, and so (ironically) enlivens me, though the surrounding ambiance is of death.

Shifting between hard, clear images and those that shimmer intriguingly, the poet now returns to the starkly clear. He shapes three questions, three images picturing parallel plights. "Where shall we go . . . Where will birds be flying . . . Where will plants find a place to rest?" The parallelism joins us—"we"—with other life forms, each created to thrive in a natural element which is being exhausted, withdrawn. "We" have been pushed to the edge of "the last frontier," the birds to "the last sky," the plants to "the last expanse of air." The linked images impress on me the unnaturalness of our fate, since the earth itself, which should be our home and our God-given ground of nurturing communal life, has been turned against us.

And so what remains for us? Only, it appears, a desperate affirmation of our identity in death: "We will write our names in crimson vapor." In the crimson I picture blood, but we have been made so insubstantial that our blood is only vaporous mist.

Another desperate act: "We will cut off the hand of song." Why am I even writing poetry (song), the poet wonders. Mere words seem futile; only "our flesh" can now speak for us, it seems. So we "dismember" ourselves, as at the start of the poem, here cutting off the hand of our voice. We give our bodies—our entire communal body—over to die, "here in the last narrow passage."

"The last narrow passage" returns us to the poem's start. The whole poem has been a funereal incantation of "lasts": "the last one of us . . . this last space of ours . . . the last frontier . . . the last sky . . . the last expanse of air." But the poem doesn't in fact end here. The poet's imagination can't, it seems, utterly bury itself. He pictures an "or," an alternative final image: "Or here our blood will plant—its olive trees." Is this an image of hope?

In Palestinian culture, the ancient olive groves are passed down through family generations. So the olive, this fruit of the earth, is a rich Palestinian symbol for the continuity of life rooted in family heritage and in land. That the poet can imagine the fruit of his people's death as olive trees does seem, then, a gesture of hope.

But for me, the poem's hope lies not so much in this final image as in the fact that Darwish managed to write the poem at all. Any creative act is a gesture of hope in violent times. Poetry's hand is cut off, yet the poem is still made; the poetic imagination still has life. In the existence of the poem itself—of any poem giving voice to any people's suffering— the people's identity is validated and given dignity. Even written in "crimson vapor," our names are at least named.

And so I might pray—

- I might pray with these lines from a poem called "Psalm," by Israeli poet Yehuda Amichai, who also wonders how poetry can go on at all in heartbreaking times:

    When I was a child I sang in the synagogue choir,
    I sang till my voice broke. I sang
    first voice and second voice. And I'll go on singing
    till my heart breaks, first heart and second heart.
    A psalm.

- I might pray with these verses from Judith Deem Dupree's epic poem, *I Sing America*, here reflecting on our early national experience of Native Americans succumbing to European intrusion. Dupree's lines seem to echo and to answer, in hope, Darwish's pained question of "Where will birds be flying, after the last sky?"

> I sing a dirge—
> To the numbing of a dying spirit.
> As of a blinded, crippled eagle.
> Feathers trailing dust.
>
> I sing a song of hope . . .
> Of wings at rest for another day's unfolding.
> Of rich brown clay kept moist
> For another year's remolding.
> I hear the ancient keening.
> A sighing on the wind, calling now—
> Stirring through the dust.

- I might pray with these lines from "An Interim" by Denise Levertov, affirming the value of those who (like Darwish) "could bear no more," who felt compelled to devote their imaginative energy to resisting the violence of their times, so that they

> Might burn through the veil that blinds
> those who do not imagine the burned bodies
> of other people's children.
>
> We need them.
> Brands that flare to show us
> the dark we are in,
> to keep us moving in it.

And, finally, I might ponder these various reflections by
Mahmoud Darwish himself, on what use poetry can have in
times of violence, particularly of war. "Against barbarity,
poetry can resist only by confirming its attachment to human
fragility like a blade of grass growing on a wall while armies
march by," he wrote on one occasion. Asked recently by an
interviewer whether he still believed that, he replied, "I
thought poetry could change everything, could change
history and could humanize, and I think that the illusion is
very necessary to push poets to be involved and to believe.
But now I think that poetry changes only the poet."
Whatever Darwish objectively thinks about poetry's
usefulness, however, as a poet he can't help but create poems.
As he put it in a poem called "Psalm 11," addressed to his
beloved countryland:

> Nothing remains for me
> But to be a vagrant in your shadow that is my shadow
> Nothing remains for me
> But to inhabit your voice that is my voice.

*Returning to the poem one more time, is there an image I want to
sit with in prayer, in hope?*

Chapter Six

'To Construct for the Buddha a Dwelling'

For three decades starting in the 1960s, poet Denise Levertov struggled to find ways that her poetry could be a force for lessening the violence of those times. In one essay on the subject, she said,

> A poetry articulating the dreads and horrors of our time is necessary in order to make readers understand what is happening, really understand it, not just know *about* it but feel it.... And a poetry of praise is equally necessary, that we not be overcome by despair but have the constant incentive of envisioned positive possibility—and because praise is an irresistible impulse of the soul.

During the 1960s, in her pain over the Vietnam War, sometimes Levertov could write only poems articulating the horrors. But in "The Altars in the Street" she found an incentive to praise. It came from a newspaper report that she cites as the poem's epigraph. Seizing on this single hope-full event, she let her poetic imagination sink into the scene, envisioning the positive possibility—and reality—of its extraordinary details.

The Altars in the Street

On June 17th, *The New York Times* reported that,
as part of the Buddhist campaign of non-violent resistance,
Vietnamese children were building altars in the streets of
Saigon and Hue, effectively jamming traffic.

Children begin at green dawn nimbly to build
topheavy altars, overweighted with prayers,
thronged each instant more densely

with almost-visible ancestors.
Where tanks have cracked the roadway
the frail altars shake; here a boy

with red stumps for hands steadies a corner,
here one adjusts with his crutch the holy base.
The vast silence of Buddha overtakes

and overrules the oncoming roar
of tragic life that fills alleys and avenues;
it blocks the way of pedicabs, police, convoys.

The hale and maimed together
hurry to construct for the Buddha
a dwelling at each intersection. Each altarmade from
    whatever stones, sticks, dreams, are at hand,
is a facet of one altar; by noon
the whole city in all its corruption,

all its shed blood the monsoon cannot wash away,
has become a temple,
fragile, insolent, absolute.

—*Denise Levertov*

How does the poem lead me to hope?

The poem hands me images of hope in its very first words. "Children," "begin," "green," "dawn," "build": these are all terms rich with the promise of renewal. The image of a green dawn is particularly intriguing. I'd expect dawn to be rose-colored or golden; by making it green, the poet fills this dawn with the color of new leaves, natural growth.

Though the children build "nimbly," a precariousness threatens their structures. The altars become "topheavy" and "overweighted" and "thronged." (These are real children that the poet is picturing, wonderfully overenthusiastic in throwing themselves into their task.) Yet what overweights the altars are "prayers" and "almost-visible ancestors": the topheavy density is of spiritual mass.

Only now, fortified by the strength of altars dense with the prayers of the dead and the living, does the poem move to meet the violent force that the altars are meant to counteract. The war becomes present to us in its effects: the roadway cracked by "tanks," a boy's "red stumps for hands," another child's "crutch." But the war isn't winning. As horrible as these images of war-maimed children are, the poet shows them upholding the frail but undaunted spiritual presence.

And then Buddha himself enters the poem to sustain the children's cause. Buddha's "vast silence" confronts the "oncoming roar / of tragic life." And it is no contest:

Buddha's silent power "overtakes" and "overrules" the din of daily war. The children's altars had been *over*weighted with prayers; now Buddha's vast silence *over*takes and *over*rules. In these images of the *over*ness of spiritual power, the poem makes concrete the divine force at the heart of nonviolent witness.

At the same time, the poet fills in the details of the scene as *The New York Times* had reported it. Morning traffic in the form of "pedicabs, police, convoys" is blocked "at each intersection" where an altar has been built. But it is the spiritual reality that continues to grip her imagination. Each altar is made of "dreams" as well as stones and sticks; each is "a dwelling" for the Buddha; each is "a facet of one altar" which calls forth the Buddha's all-encompassing presence.

And "by noon" she has the final images of her face-off. On the one hand there is war's totality of evil: "the whole city in *all* its corruption, / *all* its shed blood the monsoon cannot wash away." On the other hand there is the power of prayer, of altars built to Buddha, which conquer the evil by transforming it totally: "the whole city . . . has become a temple, / fragile, insolent, absolute."

So hope has the poem's last word, as it did the first. War in the poem is literally enveloped by something yet stronger than violence: the transformative force of prayer-filled nonviolent resistance. Even the strongest force of nature— the monsoon's winds and rains—"cannot wash away" war's bloodshed. But the sticks and stones and dreams of mere maimed children can do this and more: can turn the battered city into a temple witnessing to Buddha's vast will over-ruling war.

The poet isn't sentimental about the transformative power of nonviolent witness. The temple is "fragile," she acknowledges. But the temple is also "insolent," a word that jolts us into recalling prayer's subversive strength: though the altars are frail, they defiantly block the way of tanks and blood. Normal "tragic life" will resume, we and the poet know. Yet she has been able to envision, for herself and for us, the way that violence is overtaken and overruled. In this way, the temple is "absolute."

And so I might pray—

- I might pray with the poem's image of constructing for the Buddha "a dwelling at each intersection." This is what we all must do, I see. At every intersection of our lives, at each crossing of violence, we must construct a dwelling for our God. What prayers should we put upon our altars?

- I might pray with the Beatitudes, which, as Thomas Merton said, "are the theological foundation of Christian nonviolence." Merton explains:

  Christian nonviolence and meekness imply a particular understanding of the power of human poverty and powerlessness when they are united with the invisible strength of Christ. The Beatitudes indeed convey a profound existential understanding of the dynamic of the Kingdom of God—a dynamic made clear in the parables of the mustard seed and of the yeast. This is a dynamism of patient and secret growth, in belief that out of the

smallest, weakest, and most insignificant seed
the greatest tree will come. . . . Christian
nonviolence is a formal profession of faith in
the Gospel message that the *Kingdom has been
established* and that the Lord of truth is indeed
risen and reigning over his Kingdom.[1]

Like the poem's Buddha, whose vast silence "overrules the
oncoming roar of tragic life."

- I might pray with Gandhi, for whom prayer was the very
  root of nonviolence, or "soul force," as he called it. "No
  human being can stop violence. God alone can do so,"
  Gandhi insisted. But with God's grace, "nonviolence is the
  greatest and most active force in the world. . . . In it
  physical incapacity is no handicap, and even a frail woman
  or a child"—even the poem's child "with red stumps for
  hands"—"can pit herself or himself on equal terms against
  a giant armed with the most powerful weapons."[2]

And, finally, I might ponder this image, from the poem "How
St. Francis Teaches Us to Open Heaven," of the daunting
challenge faced by those who pit the force of God's love
alone against an enemy's power. Franciscan poet Murray
Bodo is recalling his childhood picture of heaven as lights
behind night's curtain:

St. Francis
said an enemy's hand was creased with
codes that told the merest boy how to
open God's bright heaven. The hidden
handle was the enemy's very hand, and

hateful eyes were openings to glory. But
how was I to know what lightless labyrinths
those creases trace, how long it takes to
travel easy there before the handle turns.

*Returning to the poem one more time, is there an image I want to
sit with in prayer, in hope?*

NOTES

[1] Thomas Merton, "Blessed Are the Meek: The Christian Roots of
Nonviolence," in *Passion for Peace: The Social Essays,* William H.
Shannon, ed. (New York: Crossroads, 1995) p. 251.

[2] Quoted in Thomas Merton, *Gandhi on Non-Violence* (New York: New
Directions, 1965), pp. 28, 31, 44.

Chapter Seven

'The Fear of It Leaves Me'

Wendell Berry is a farmer and a prolific writer of novels, essays and poems. In all his work, whether with plough or pen, he indefatigably seeks ways for us to live in harmony: with one another in community and with our natural environment. Over twenty years ago, Berry began composing what he calls his Sabbath Poems. Written out of doors in solitude and silence, they are meditations on the meaning of Sabbath rest. He titles the poems simply by numbering them during the course of a year. Here is the one he places first in the published collection that he named *A Timbered Choir*.

1979:1

I go among trees and sit still.
All my stirring becomes quiet
around me like circles on water.
My tasks lie in their places
where I left them, asleep like cattle.

Then what is afraid of me comes
and lives a while in my sight.
What it fears in me leaves me,
and the fear of me leaves it.
It sings, and I hear its song.

Then what I am afraid of comes.
I live for a while in its sight.
What I fear in it leaves it,
and the fear of it leaves me.
It sings, and I hear its song.

After days of labor,
mute in my consternations,
I hear my song at last,
and I sing it. As we sing,
the day turns, the trees move.

—*Wendell Berry*

How does the poem lead me to hope?

Just reading through this poem is a calming experience. Even
apart from the images of stillness, of release from tensed up
fear, the pacing has a quieting effect. Each line has a feel of
three soft beats with no rush between, but rather a hushed
lightness, as if the poem is moving on tiptoe. The

deliberately simple vocabulary—most words are one syllable—and the many repetitions give the sense of a liturgical chant.

"I go among trees and sit still." The setting and the entire action of the poem are already contained in the opening line. The rest is simply ripple effect. I've come to this Sabbath moment naturally carrying the week's "stirrings," but they ripple away "like circles on water." Because I "sit still," nothing disturbs my workaday preoccupations, so they are allowed to lie quiet, "asleep like cattle."

"Then" the most extraordinary thing happens. Because I "sit still"—because, that is, I'm not fussing around self-importantly—"what is afraid of me" is freed to come near. Maybe it is a bird, hopping up close to the tranquil human presence. Because I continue to "sit still"—because, that is, I make no gesture to startle it—the bird stays and "lives a while in my sight." And in its trusting presence, any instinct I might have had to disturb it dissolves, so that the bird's instinct to fear me dissolves in return. Utterly at comfort in my sight, "it sings, and I hear its song."

In composing this stanza, though, the poet has been careful not to name "what is afraid of me." Whether or not a bird or other woodland creature actually came before him as he sat still among the trees, he clearly experiences the transaction more generally. He keeps all the language for the transaction open, loose, large—so that "what is afraid of me" *might* be a small wild creature, but it might also be a person over whom I have power, or (if "I" am a powerful corporation or nation) a whole population that lives subject to my control.

My experience of the stanza, then, is open to whatever truly is, in my life, "afraid of me." Experiencing the stanza in this openness, something even more extraordinary happens. Because I "sit still"—because, that is, I'm not gearing up to attack it—*whatever* "is afraid of me" is freed to come near. Not feeling threatened by me (again, because I "sit still"), it quietly "lives a while in my sight." And because we "sit still" now together, seeing each other "a while" up close, "what it fears in me" (maybe my manipulativeness, my bullying, my superior wealth which can buy up and control its resources) "leaves me." That is, I'm the one who is changed, freed from behaviors that cause fear in others, so that the other then feels its fear melt away. Freed from fear of me, it naturally "sings," it celebrates life, and I'm freed to "hear" its song, to let its celebration touch my soul. Gandhi once wrote, "Fear of the foreigner is what gives rise to hatred. Fear gone, there can be no hatred. Thus his conversion implies our conversion too."[1]

"Then" another extraordinary thing happens, as the third stanza recounts. Because I "sit still," letting "all my stirring" about my own supposed needs and tasks settle down, "what I am afraid of" is freed to come out into the open. Maybe it is literally a wild animal; maybe it is my recognition of a person or group who frightens me. In any case, because I'm in the Sabbath mind-set of letting be, letting rest, I let myself "live for a while," simply gazing at what I feel threatened by. And after a while, "what I fear in it" (maybe its raucous disruption of my way of life, its threat to my comforts, its competing for my job) "leaves it." That is, it is changed by the dissolving of my fear, so that my fear loses its object. Instead of rattling sabers, what I was afraid of now "sings" a joy of life that I am open now to sharing. Merton once wrote: "The only way truly to 'overcome' an enemy is to help him become other than an enemy."[2]

The whole poem is a parable. The "days of labor" are all my obsessings over my own agenda, whether the laboring "I" is my individual self or my political interest group or my nation. Our self-protective "consternations" (the poem's only multi-syllable word, looking and sounding exactly like the overdone fussing that it is) have kept us mute: unable to speak or hear even our own heart's longing to rejoice. But now that I and whoever I define negatively as "other" have been freed from mutual fear, "I hear my song at last, / and I sing it." And after eighteen and a half lines of separated "I" and "it," finally "we" are singing. Immediately, "as we sing," nature responds in harmony. The trees that had first moved me to stillness now "move" in tune with our song.

"All the trees of the forest sing for joy before the LORD; for he is coming." So sings Psalm 96 (the psalms are songs). God's presence in our hearts is the Sabbath's gift. Or rather, God is always present, but the gift of Sabbath stillness allows us to settle into the trust of truly knowing this. "Be still," sings Psalm 46, "and know that I am God!"

If "we" everywhere, all of us in God's creation, prayed this poem deeply and sincerely every day—making every day a Sabbath rest from mutual fear—how could we possibly sustain our violence against one another?

And so I might pray—

- I might pray with this reflection by essayist Richard Rodriguez:

In 1492 when the Indians saw the Spanish
galleon on the horizon, they did not run to
their ethnic studies departments in fear. They
came to the edge of the water to wait. In the
history of ideas, there is no more moving, no
more touching moment than that: that
strangers, complete and utter strangers,
would not be afraid of each other but would
be drawn by their differences.[3]

- I might pray that I can bring myself to share Pope John
  XXIII's hope, expressed in his encyclical *Pacem in Terris*
  (¶129), during the violent times of the nuclear arms race:

  There is reason to hope that by meeting and
  negotiating, people may come to discover
  better the bonds—deriving from the human
  nature which they have in common—that
  unite them, and that they may learn also that
  one of the most profound requirements of
  their common nature is this: that between
  them and their respective peoples it is not fear
  which should reign but love, a love which
  tends to express itself in a collaboration that is
  loyal, manifold in form, and productive of
  many benefits.

- I might pray with these lines from the poem "Jerusalem,"
  by Arab-American poet Naomi Shihab Nye:

  There's a place in this brain
  where hate won't grow.
  I touch its riddle: wind, and seeds.
  Something pokes us as we sleep.

And, finally, I might ponder the experience I had during the late 1980s, when I decided to go live for a while in the sight of what I most feared at the time: our nation's build-up of nuclear weapons. So I rented out my upstate New York home for a year and moved to New Mexico, close by the Los Alamos laboratory where nuclear weapons were being designed out of fear of the Soviet nuclear arsenal. I introduced myself to the laboratory's scientists and administrators as someone frankly representing what they were afraid of on the domestic front: the nuclear disarmament movement. But I said, truly, that I had come among them not to argue or to demonstrate but to listen: to open my mind and heart to the fears that motivated them to devote their lives to creating what to me were the most fearful of human inventions. After living for a while this way in each other's sight, we began to be able to hear each other's song: the hopes in each of our hearts. I never stopped fearing the terrible threat of nuclear disaster, nor did they, but I stopped demonizing the weapons designers in my mind, stopped belittling their own way of responding to that fear. And we even came, occasionally, to sing together: they graciously invited me into their homes for meals, for real fellowship.

Returning to the poem one more time, is there an image I want to sit with in prayer, in hope?

NOTES
[1] Quoted in Thomas Merton, *Gandhi on Non-Violence*, p. 41.
[2] Ibid., p. 15.
[3] Richard Rodriguez, interviewed in *Image #34* (Spring 2002), p. 59.

Chapter Eight

'The Saints Pelt Us with Flowers'

Jesuit priest Daniel Berrigan, poet and peace activist, served
many jail sentences for acts of civil disobedience protesting
his nation's wars and weapons. In his poetry, he often takes
on the voice of the biblical prophets, who swing between
castigating their society for its misdeeds and calling it to the
harmonious relations that are God's hope for us. As both
poet and activist, Berrigan shares the biblical prophets' goal
of moving us to reform (indeed re-form, re-shape) our society
into one that embodies God's love. Poetry is a medium
especially suited to move us in this manner, since it can show
the imagination at work in the very process of reenvisioning
our world. Biblical prophecy itself is in fact often called
"poetic" because it uses language similarly, proliferating
images of the transformation of violence into harmony. But
neither prophecy nor poetry tries to *force* us to reform. What
they do is offer transformative images so alluring that we
long to live them out.

Swords into Plowshares

Everything enhances, everything
gives glory—everything!

Between bark and bite
Judge Salus's undermined soul
betrays him, mutters
very alleluias.

The iron cells—
row on row of rose trellised
mansions, bridal chambers!

Curses, vans, keys, guards—behold
the imperial lions of our vast acres!

And when hammers come down
and our years are tossed to four winds—

why, flowers blind the eye, the saints
pelt us with flowers!

For every hour
scant with discomfort
(the mastiff's baleful eye,
the bailiff's mastery)—

see, the Lord's hands heap
eon upon eon,
like fruit bowls at a feast.

—*Daniel Berrigan*

How does the poem lead me to hope?

The poem's title sets up my expectations, by quoting the well-known image from Isaiah 2:4 and Micah 4:3. This must be the most popular prophetic image that we have for the nearly universal longing to transform any war-making culture into one that cultivates peace. So familiar is the biblical passage from which the image comes (it is a standard during Advent and at prayer services for peace in times of violent conflict between nations) that these three words bring to mind the whole prophetic oracle. God himself, the prophet asserts, "shall judge between the nations" as their arbiter. "They shall beat their swords into plowshares, and their spears into pruning hooks; nation shall not lift up sword against nation, neither shall they learn war any more." Isaiah's version then exhorts: "O house of Jacob, come, let us walk in the light of the LORD!" And Berrigan's poem follows as if it were a resounding "Yes! Let's heed the prophet's call! Let's see what happens if we do truly walk in the light of the Lord."

And immediately what happens is that the light of the Lord glorifies "everything . . . everything . . . everything!" There could hardly be a more all-embracing opening to a poem. The poet plays with the grammar and line-break to expand the glorifying force of "everything" even further. "Everything enhances," adds value and beauty to its very self. Yet more: "everything enhances, everything," making the second everything the fortunate object of the first's enhancement, so that each and every thing shines back on the other in an infinitely enhancing mutual mirroring. Yet this second "everything" spills over into the next line, where it "gives glory." Then with a dash all this enhancing and glorifying activity is swept up into a third exclamatory "everything!" Walking in the light of the Lord has brought us right into the midst of a trinitarian dynamism of celebratory joy.

Through the rest of the poem, the poet simply takes literally this opening vision. He looks at certain things—some specifics of his trial and prison experience—which on the surface don't appear glorious at all. Yet as soon as he shines on them the light of the Lord, they do give utterly unexpected glory—to the wonder of all involved.

A judge with an evidently gruff manner finds his soul "undermined" by the creative subversion of the Holy Spirit, so that (despite himself) his snarls come out of his mouth as "alleluias."

The poet's prison bars are turned, by the force of his imagination, into "row on row of rose trellises," with the cells enhanced into "mansions," even "bridal chambers" for love's celebration.

"Curses, vans, keys, guards"—each bit of the hard experience of arrest—"behold"! In the light of the Lord, the poet sees them shining in expansive joy as the noble creatures of his vast domain, the kingdom of God.

The poet's years serving prison sentences: are they lost years to be mourned? No! They are years lightly "tossed to four winds." And in the hammer pounding out each of the jail sentences over the years, "the saints pelt us with flowers!" What an image of the transformation of violence into joyful hope. As the poet puts his imagination to work (to play) glorifying "everything . . . everything," the light of the Lord becomes a lightness of spirit, a light-hearted exuberance, which diffuses violence by absorbing its hammer-blows and transmitting them back as flowering delight.

And now, for the final two stanzas, the poet pulls away for an overview of his life of voluntary submission to the judicial system. From the imaginative distance that poetry allows him, he sees both his discomfort and time itself transformed. The discomforts he suffered had constricted time, making every hour seem "scant." Playfully, he represents the sense of confinement by tight punning squeezed inside a parenthesis, where guard dogs and court guardians are menacingly interchangeable. In the context, the parenthesis looks confining, like a jail cell; yet it also limits and subordinates the horror of the years-long experience, making it merely parenthetical.

Full liberation comes, however, only through full re-envisioning. But "see," the poet exhorts himself and us. See what is really going on in each of these oppressive hours, if we only look in the light(ness) of the Lord. We see the gift of grace abounding: "the Lord's hands heap eon upon eon, like fruit bowls at a feast."

The poem has turned swords into plowshares, over and over again, before our eyes.

And so I might pray—

- I might pray with the creatively imaginative overturnings of Romans 12:14–21: "Bless those who persecute you; bless and do not curse them. . . . Do not repay anyone evil for evil. . . . No, 'if your enemies are hungry, feed them; if they are thirsty, give them something to drink; for by doing this you will heap burning coals on their heads.' Do not be overcome by evil, but overcome evil with good"— and with fun.

- I might pray with these surahs of the Qu'ran: "Good deeds and evil deeds are not equal. Requite evil with good, and he who is your enemy will become your dearest friend" (41:34). "True servants of the Merciful are those who walk humbly on the earth and say 'Peace!' to the ignorant who accost them" (25:63).

- I might pray with William Stafford's poem "Peace Walk," which invites us to place our bodies as signs of hope even though violence (here, the danger of nuclear explosive fallout) might seem to be prevailing:

  > We wondered what our walk should mean,
  > taking that un-march quietly;
  > the sun stared at our signs—"Thou shalt not kill" . . .

  > Above our heads the sound truck blared—
  > by the park, under the autumn trees—
  > it said that love could fill the atmosphere:

  > Occur, slow the other fallout, unseen,
  > on islands everywhere—fallout, falling
  > unheard. We held our poster up to shade our eyes.

And, finally, I might ponder what theologian James Alison writes, in *Faith Beyond Resentment*, about how those of us who feel victimized by systemic violence will know that the Spirit of God has come upon us. It will be

> when we are not even bothered or scandalised by church authorities, angry preachers, hypocritical politicians and so on, because we are too busy doing our own thing. And our own thing, if we really have learned to inhabit the biblical story, will be to see beyond the anger and the hatred and the violence in the hearts of those we once saw as our persecutors, over against whom we railed with similar anger, hatred and violence as we held on to our indignant and tense identities. Instead we will be learning to reach out to the brothers, hidden under the guise of hypocrites, cowards and traitors who do not yet dare to become unscandalised by the adventure of creation.[1]

Returning to the poem one more time, is there an image I want to sit with in prayer, in hope?

NOTES
[1] James Alison, *Faith Beyond Resentment* (New York: Crossroad, 2001), p. 206.

Chapter Nine
'Like a Tree over the Sleeper'

Israel's leading modern poet, Yehuda Amichai, lived his
entire life amid violence. Born into a German Jewish home
in 1924, he fled the Nazis in the 1930s, settling with his
family in what was then Palestine. He fought in World War II
and in the Israeli War of Independence. For most of his
adulthood, until his death in 2000, he lived in the conflict-
ridden city of Jerusalem. Yet somehow, through it all, he
managed to write poems that express a gentle spirit and a
love of humanity. So universal is the appeal of his poetry
that it has been translated into thirty-seven languages,
making him (his fans say jokingly) the most widely
translated Hebrew poet since King David, to whom the
psalms are attributed. In Amichai's poetry, any hope offered
us comes through hard experience.

God Has Pity on Kindergarten Children

God has pity on children in kindergartens,
He pities school children—less.
But adults he pities not at all.

He abandons them,
Sometimes they have to crawl on all fours
In the roasting sand
To reach the dressing station,
and they are streaming with blood.

But perhaps
He will have pity on those who love truly
And take care of them
And shade them,
Like a tree over the sleeper on the public bench.

Perhaps even we will spend on them
Our last pennies of kindness
Inherited from mother,

So that their own happiness will protect us
Now and on other days.

—*Yehuda Amichai*

How does the poem lead me to hope?

At first, the poem seems to be draining me of hope rather than leading me toward it. Though the opening line does offer hope in the form of God's pity—the loving kindness (*hesed*) poured out by God in so many of the psalms—hope steadily shrinks as the stanza goes on. As people grow older, God pities them less and less. Such is the poet's stark vision, literalized by the diminishing length of each line as God's pity is withdrawn.

Until the line is shrunk to three terrifying words: "He abandons them." I hear Psalm 22: "My God, my God, why have you forsaken me?" I see, through the remaining lines of this second stanza, the vivid image that the poet provides of war's victims: adults reduced to crawling like helpless babies "streaming with blood." It is the low point of the poem, the low point of the human condition: people dragging their violently wounded bodies over the hostile earth's "roasting sand." This single dreadful image cries out with all humankind's anguished question in times of violence: where is God in this horror?

"But perhaps": with these two words, I hold my breath expectantly. "Perhaps" is a word of hope, of the possibility of some alternative to utter abandonment by God. And hope's content comes in the next line: "Perhaps," the poet suggests, God "will have pity on those who love truly."

At once, with the possibility that there do exist "those who love truly," the stanza flows on into the loveliest of images of care (especially in a climate of roasting sand): being "shade" for others, "like a tree over the sleeper on the public bench." The long, expansive line visually stretches out its protective loving care. In my mind's eye, too, the line's protectiveness glides into the image of the righteous persons in Psalm 1, who are "like trees planted by streams of water." In my mind's eye, further, the line's protectiveness glides into the image of God as our "keeper" in Psalm 121:

"The LORD is your shade at your right hand. The sun shall not strike you by day."

In the psalms, the righteous are strongly protective, like trees; and so is God. And in the poem? Can I tell who exactly is "like a tree"? Is it "those who love truly"? Or is it "He" (God)? I look back over the stanza to check its grammar, and find that the answer must be: both. The grammatical subject of "take care of them and shade them" could be "He"; in this case, "them" could be either "those who love truly" or those he had abandoned to crawl on all fours in their own blood. But the subject of "take care of them and shade them" could equally be "those who love truly," in the sense that "those who love truly and take care of" the helpless war victims are pitied (blessed) by God.

This grammatical ambiguity has an odd and challenging effect. God's care of us seems to merge with—maybe even depend on—our care for one another. Once there are "those who love truly," the poem suggests, God's pity and caretaking can operate *through* them, directly through their acts of lovingkindness. Hope is returning to the poem, but it is hope placed in *us*.

The poet goes on to elaborate this hope, but tentatively— with another "perhaps"—as if he can't be sure yet how much we can be counted on (though without us, it's becoming clear, hope fades). "Perhaps even we . . ." Here, unequivocally, "we" become the acting subject on whom kindness depends. And as "we" formally enter the poem, God seems to exit; the poem doesn't mention him again. God's disappearance, however, is only apparent; his blessing remains over each of our own self-giving acts. For we all have *something* to give, the poet implies in the image of "our last pennies of kindness / Inherited from mother." If we spend, expend, our loving care on those bleeding with need, "their own happiness will protect us / Now and on other days."

These closing lines have the sound of a psalm. "God will protect your going out and your coming in, now and forever," the psalmist often ends. Except that the poet has given God's place to us people—not in arrogance, but in a vision of our mutual responsibility for one another's happiness. This is the responsibility that we grow into as adults. When we abandon it, we are left like the "adults" at the poem's start: abandoned by God, because we have abandoned ourselves. God abandons us to one another.

We ourselves, the poem quietly hints, are one another's hope in violent times.

And so I might pray—

- I might pray with this famous passage from the Qur'an, where God challenges those of us of different faiths—Jews and Christians and Muslims—to compete with each other not in argument or with arms but in acts of goodness. Speaking of himself, God says that he has ". . . ordained a law and assigned a path for each of you. Had God pleased, He could have made of you one community: but it is His wish to prove you by that which He has bestowed upon you. Vie with each other in good works, for to God shall you all return" (5:49).

- I might pray with these lines from Nobel Prize poet Nelly Sachs, a German Jew who—after escaping Nazi persecution—devoted her poetry to probing the implications of the Holocaust. Surely *someone*, she writes in hope, in prayer,

Someone
will take the ball
from the hands that play
the game of terror. . . .

Someone will come
and sew the green of the spring bud
on their prayer shawl
and set the child's silken curl
as a sign
on the brow the century . . .

• I might pray with this verse from "For the 500th Dead
Palestinian, Ibtisam Bozieh," by Arab-American poet
Naomi Shihab Nye:

How do we carry the endless surprise
of all our deaths? Becoming doctors
for one another, Arab, Jew,
instead of guarding tumors of pain
as if they hold us upright?

And, finally, I might ponder these words by Archbishop of
Canterbury Rowan Williams, who happened to be in New
York for a conference near the World Trade Center on
September 11, 2001:

The morning after, I was stopped in the street
in New York by a youngish man who turned
out to be an airline pilot and a Catholic. He
wanted to know what the hell God was doing
when the planes hit the towers. What do you

say? The usual fumbling about how God doesn't intervene, which sounds like a lame apology for some kind of "policy" on God's part, a policy exposed as heartless in the face of such suffering? Something about how God is there in the sacrificial work of the rescuers, in the risks they take? I tried saying bits of this, but there was no clearer answer than there ever is. Any really outrageous human action tests to the limit our careful theological principles about God's refusal to interfere with created freedom. . . . He has made the world so that evil choices can't just be frustrated or aborted (where would he stop, for goodness sake? he'd have to be intervening every instant of human history) but have to be confronted, suffered, taken forward, healed in the complex process of human history, always in collaboration with what we do and say and pray.[1]

Returning to the poem one more time, is there an image I want to sit with in prayer, in hope?

NOTES
[1] Rowan Williams, *Writing in the Dust* (Grand Rapids, Mich.: Eerdmans, 2002), pp. 7–8.

Chapter Ten
'Bare Feet, Face, and Nothing Hidden'

"Imagining is an act of hope," writes Professor Janine Langan in her essay "The Christian Imagination."[1] What she means is that, through the amazing gift of the imagination, God bestows on us the capacity to "challenge fate" and to join in God's ongoing creative activity in our world. Poetry itself is this creative activity embodied in language; poetry is the play of imagination in words. And who in Christian history embodies God's engaging creativity better than Saint Francis? So it is right in the spirit of both poetry's play and Saint Francis' witness that contemporary U.S. poet Maren Tirabassi composed her poem "St. Francis." Opening up the famous peace prayer attributed to Francis, Tirabassi plays off each line of the prayer by inserting an image of its literal embodiment.

St. Francis
Lord,
make me a means
of your

open hands.

Where there is hatred let me sow

open smile.

Let me not so much
seek to be understood,
as to

open eyes,

to be comforted
as to
be still.

For it is in forgiving
that we are

face upturned,

and it is in dying that

*we who are most foolish,
open and yet full
(hands, smile, eyes,
heart),*

*with our big ears and
fat lips and an Adam's apple bobbing
and rags for robes*

*and bare feet,
face,
and nothing hidden, not even
the God inside
are born, born . . .*
we are born to everlasting life.

—Maren Tirabassi

How does the poem lead me to hope?

Saint Francis was the very *embodiment* of joyful hope. He *embraced* with passionate delight every encounter that life brought him. The famous stories about him tell of his joyfully embracing Lady Poverty, who is the spirit of dispossession; of his rushing to embrace the leper, who represents the outsider whom we feel repelled and frightened by; of his embracing with honor and respect Brother Wind and Sister Water and all the other sacred elements of God's creation. *Embrace*— that welcoming wrapping of one's whole being around everything, including pain and apparent danger or loss—this is Saint Francis to the core.

The prayer "Lord, make me an instrument of your peace" was actually composed centuries after Francis' life. But it is so true to his spirit that it could indeed have come from his mouth. And it is so well known that Tirabassi needs only to touch on a few words of each petition in order for the rest to pop up before our minds. At the instant when our minds are completing the petition, however, she gives us a concrete bodily image to picture what we are praying for: *open hands* as the prayer's "peace," *open smile* as its "love," *open eyes* as its "understanding," *face upturned* as its forgiveness.

If we read down through the poem's italicized lines alone, we get a portrait of the human being who embodies every gesture of God's peace. It is a portrait of who we are praying to be, as we pray to conform our lives to the model of Saint Francis, who formed his life in the image of Christ.

The poem's portrait is deliberately a bit silly, for we humans are truly "most foolish." We hope that it is for Christ, though, that we (with Saint Paul) are fools; we hope that it is for God's delight that we fling ourselves exuberantly (with Saint Francis) into dying to self. The poet provides an endearing picture of us, "with our big ears and fat lips and an Adam's apple bobbing"—like happy children of Adam, bobbing for apples in messy splashing play.

"Rags for robes / and bare feet": here we are, now, adorned in the garb of Saint Francis. With him, we "put on Christ" (as Saint Paul exhorts), stripping ourselves bare of defenses, self-deceptions, self-justifications, until we remain with "nothing hidden, not even"—the poet teasingly makes us wait a line for the glorious revelation—"the God inside."

In writing this poem, Tirabassi was meditating on a statue of Saint Francis made by the sculptor Charles McCollough. We don't need to see the sculpture, though, to see embodied in the poem Francis' wholehearted way of throwing himself into God's life in Christ. "Lord, make me a means of *your* open hands," the poem begins. Let your every gesture of extravagant love be mine.

As we pray the poem, we join with Saint Francis. Through the poem's images, we pray to be—in our own bodies and beings—Christ's own hatred-dissolving love, Christ's own forgiveness, Christ's own reconciling peace. "For he is our peace," Ephesians 2:13–16 reminds us; "in his flesh" he has made us all one, creating "in himself one new humanity," reconciling all of us to one another and to God through his cross.

With Tirabassi's "St. Francis," we can literally pray through poetry—through poetry's special way of engaging us in its images—to hope. In violent times, in all times.

And so I might pray—

- I might pray with the biblical figure of Wisdom personified, who is "a breath of the power of God, and a pure emanation of the glory of the Almighty. . . . In every generation she passes into holy souls and makes them friends of God and prophets" (Wisdom 7:25–27).

- I might pray with these lines from the poem "The Little Flowers of Saint Francis," by Franciscan Father Murray Bodo. The Little Flowers are the early stories of Saint Francis' wildly exuberant acts of dispossession and of total trust in God.

> Mainly they are feet,
> these stories, and a tripping
> movement light with
> what they do not carry. . . .
> And you,
> Francis, oboe of God,
> silly of finger and lip,
> somber of breath big
> with pressure held back. . . .
> The feet pluck the strings
> that hold the world together.
> See the folk tapping

to your unconscious tunes. . . .
The lift and drop of feet
unshod is scoring
the regimented march
into a counter-dance,
a coda of feet in a ring.

• I might pray with Saint Francis' exhortation to his
  brothers: "Take up your bodies and carry Christ's holy cross
  and follow His most holy commands even to the end."[2]

And, finally, I might ponder this delightful image of embodied
hope from *The Portal of the Mystery of Hope*, a book-length
poetic meditation by the early twentieth-century French
poet Charles Péguy. Imagining God as speaking, Péguy
personifies the theological virtue of hope as a little girl "who
forever begins." In humanity's fragility, God says, "absolutely
nothing at all holds"—

—except because of the young child
Hope,
Because of she who continually begins again and
    who always promises,
Who guarantees everything.
Who assures tomorrow to today and this
    afternoon to this morning.
and life to life and even eternity to time....

Young days from old days
New water from used water . . .
Fresh souls from old souls . . .
Rising souls from setting souls . . .

It's from impure water that she makes an eternal
    spring...
The eternal spring of my grace itself.
She knows well that she'll never run out of it.
My grace must, indeed, be great...

And the poet goes on to imagine a Corpus Christi
procession, with the child Hope dancing along, ahead of all
the other virtues:

She's never tired...
She's twenty steps ahead of them, like a little
    puppy, she comes back, she leaves again, she
    makes the trip twenty times.
She has fun with the garlands in the procession.

...She plays by jumping on top of the foliage...
She doesn't listen to anything. She doesn't stay
    in place during the stations.
She'd rather keep marching. Keep moving ahead.
Keep jumping. Keep dancing. She's so happy.

*Returning to the poem one more time, is there an image I want to
sit with in prayer, in hope?*

NOTES
[1] Janine Langan, "The Christian Imagination," in *The Christian Imagination:
The Practice of Faith in Literature and Writing*, Leland Ryken, ed. (Colorado
Springs, Colo.: Howard Shaw Publishers, 2002), p. 65.
[2] Quoted in "Francis of Assisi: A Symbol of Peace, " by Jay M. Hammond,
America, May 6, 2002, p. 17.

Sources of Poems
Quoted or Mentioned

Amichai, Yehuda. "God Has Pity on Kindergarten Children."
Poems. Translated by Assia Gutmann. New York: Harper
& Row, 1969.

——————. "Psalm." *The Selected Poetry of Yehuda Amichai*.
Translated by Chana Bloch and Stephen Mitchell. New
York: Harper & Row, 1986.

Berrigan, Daniel. "Swords into Plowshares." *And the Risen
Bread: Selected Poems, 1957–1997*, edited by John Dear.
New York: Fordham University Press, 1998.

Berry, Wendell. "1979:1." *A Timbered Choir: The Sabbath
Poems 1979–1997*. Boulder, Colo.: Counterpoint Press,
1998.

——————. "Manifesto: The Mad Farmer Liberation Front."
The Collected Poems, 1957-1982. San Francisco: North
Point Press, 1987.

Bodo, Murray. "How St. Francis Teaches Us to Open
Heaven" and "The Little Flowers of Saint Francis." *Icarus
in Assisi*. Assisi: Editrice Minerva, 2002.

Cairns, Scott. "The Translation of Raimundo Luz: My
Imitation." *Philokalia*. Lincoln, Neb.: Zoo Press, 2002.

Clifton, Lucille. "adam and eve" and "cain." *Good Woman:
Poems and a Memoir 1969–1980*. Rochester, N.Y.: BOA
Editions, 1987.

Darwish, Mahmoud. "Earth Scrapes Us." Translated by Lena
Jayyusi and Christopher Middleton. *Modern Arabic
Poetry: An Anthology*. Edited by Salma Khadra Jayyusi.
New York: Columbia University Press, 1987.

————. "Psalm 11." *The Music of Human Flesh: Poems of the Palestinian Struggle*. Selected and translated by Denys Johnson-Davies. Washington, D.C.: Three Continents Press, 1980.

Dupree, Judith Deem. *I Sing America*. Pine Valley, Calif.: Quiddity Press, 2002.

Hirshfield, Jane. "October 20, 1983" and "On the Current Events." *Of Gravity and Angels*. Middletown, Conn.: Wesleyan University Press, 1988.

Levertov, Denise. "The Altars in the Street." *The Sorrow Dance*. New York: New Directions, 1967.

————. "An Interim." *Relearning the Alphabet*. New York: New Directions, 1970.

————. "Making Peace." *Breathing the Water*. New York: New Directions, 1987.

————. "Writing in the Dark." *Candles in Babylon*. New York: New Directions, 1982.

Milosz, Czeslaw. "Ars Poetica?" *The Collected Poems*. Hopewell, N.J.: Ecco Press, 1988.

Nye, Naomi Shihab. "Jerusalem" and "For the 500th Dead Palestinian, Ibtisam Bozieh" and "Passing the Refugee Camp." *19 Varieties of Gazelle*. New York: HarperCollins, 2002.

Péguy, Charles. *The Portal of the Mystery of Hope*. Translated by David Louis Schindler, Jr. Grand Rapids, Mich.: Eerdmans, 1986.

Sachs, Nelly, "Someone Will Take the Ball." *O the Chimneys: Selected Poems.* Translated by Ruth and Matthew Mead and Michael Roloff. New York: Farrar Straus Giroux, 1967.

Stafford, William. "For the Unknown Enemy" and "Peace Walk." *The Way It Is.* Saint Paul, Minn.: Graywolf Press, 1998.

Tirabassi, Maren. "St. Francis." *Faith Made Visible.* By Charles McCollough and Maren Tirabassi. Cleveland, Ohio: United Church Press, 2000.

Thomas, R. S. "The Coming." *Poems of R. S. Thomas.* Fayetteville, Ark.: University of Arkansas Press, 1985.

Williams, William Carlos. "Asphodel, That Greeny Flower." *The Collected Poems of William Carlos Williams*, Vol. II. New York: New Directions, 2001.

Zagajewski, Adam. "The Greenhouse." *Mysticism for Beginners.* Translated by Clare Cavanagh New York: Farrar, Straus & Giroux, 1998.

We are grateful for permission to quote material printed by the following publishers:

Reprinted by permission of Farrar, Straus and Giroux, "The Green House," by Adam Zagajewski, from *Mysticism for Beginners*, Clare Cavanaugh, translator, copyright ©1998. Reprinted by permission of BOA Editions, Ltd., "adam and eve" and "cain," by Lucille Clifton, from *Good Woman: Poems and a Memoir*, copyright ©1987. Reprinted by permission of Zoo Press, "The Translation of Raimundo Luz: My Imitation," by Scott Cairns, from *Philokalia*, copyright ©2002. Reprinted by permission of Wesleyan University Press, "On the Current Events," by Jane Hirshfield, from *Of Gravity and Angels*, copyright ©1988. Reprinted by permission of Columbia University Press, "Earth Scrapes Us," by Mahmoud Darwish, from *Modern Arabic Poetry: An Anthology*, Salma Khadra Jayyusi, editor, copyright ©1987. Reprinted by permission of New Directions Publishing, "The Altars in the Street," by Denise Levertov, from *Poems 1960-1967*, copyright ©1966. Reprinted by permission of Perseus Books Group, "1979:1," by Wendell Berry, from *A Timbered Choir: Sabbath Poems*, copyright ©1998. Reprinted by permission of Fordham University Press, "Swords Into Plowshares," by Daniel Berrigan, from *And the Risen Bread: Selected Poems 1957-1997*, John Dear, editor, copyright ©1998. Reprinted by permission of HarperCollins Publishers, "God Has Pity on Kindergarten Children," by Yehuda Amichai, from *Poems*, copyright ©1968. Reprinted by permission of the author and United Church Press, "St. Francis," by Maren Tirabassi, from *Faith Made Visible*, copyright ©2000.